# Symphony No. 9
## in E Minor, Op. 95

("From the New World")

# Antonín Dvořák

## DOVER PUBLICATIONS, INC.
Mineola, New York

Published in Canada by General Publishing Company, Ltd., 30 Lesmill Road, Don Mills, Toronto, Ontario.

Published in the United Kingdom by Constable and Company, Ltd., 3 The Lanchesters, 162–164 Fulham Palace Road, London W6 9ER.

### Bibliographical Note

This Dover edition, first published in 1997, is an unabridged republication of *Aus der neuen Welt. "Z nového světa." Symphonie (No. 5, E moll.) für grosses Orchester, Op. 95. Partitur,* originally published by N. Simrock, Berlin, 1894.

*International Standard Book Number: 0-486-29892-2*

Manufactured in the United States of America
Dover Publications, Inc., 31 East 2nd Street, Mineola, N.Y. 11501

# CONTENTS

## Symphony No. 9*
### in E Minor, Op. 95

### ("From the New World")

### (1893)

I. Adagio—Allegro molto     1

II. Largo     25

III. *Scherzo:* Molto vivace     35

IV. Allegro con fuoco     51

*originally published as Symphony No. 5

# INSTRUMENTATION

2 Flutes  [Flauti, Flauto gr.]
  *Flute II doubles Piccolo* [Fl. Piccolo]
2 Oboes  [Oboi]
  *Oboe II doubles English Horn*
    [Corno inglese, C. ingl.]
2 Clarinets in A, B♭("B") [Clarinetti]
2 Bassoons  [Fagotti]

4 Horns in C, E, F  [Corni]
2 Trumpets in C, E♭("Es"), E  [Trombe]
2 Trombones  [Tromboni]
Bass Trombone  [Trombone basso]
Tuba  [Tuba]

Timpani  [Tympani]
  *(Tunings "Des, Es, As, H" = D-flat, E-flat, A-flat, B)*

Percussion
  Triangle  [Triangolo]
  Cymbals  [Piatti]

Violins I, II  [Violino/i]
Violas  [Viola/e]
Cellos  [Violoncello, Celli]
Basses  [Contrabasso]

# Symphony No. 9

## in E Minor, Op. 95

### ("From the New World")

1

3

5

6

14

18

24

# II.

25

30

110
Oboi.
in B.
Solo.
molto cresc.
Tutti.
dimin.
Solo.
Tutti.
Tutti.
Solo.
Tutti.
Tutti.
molto cresc.
118
ritard.
in tempo
ritard.
Molto Adagio.
dim.
in E. a 2.
a 2.
ritard.
in tempo
ritard.
Molto Adagio.
dim.
dim.
dim.
dim.

## III. Scherzo.

35

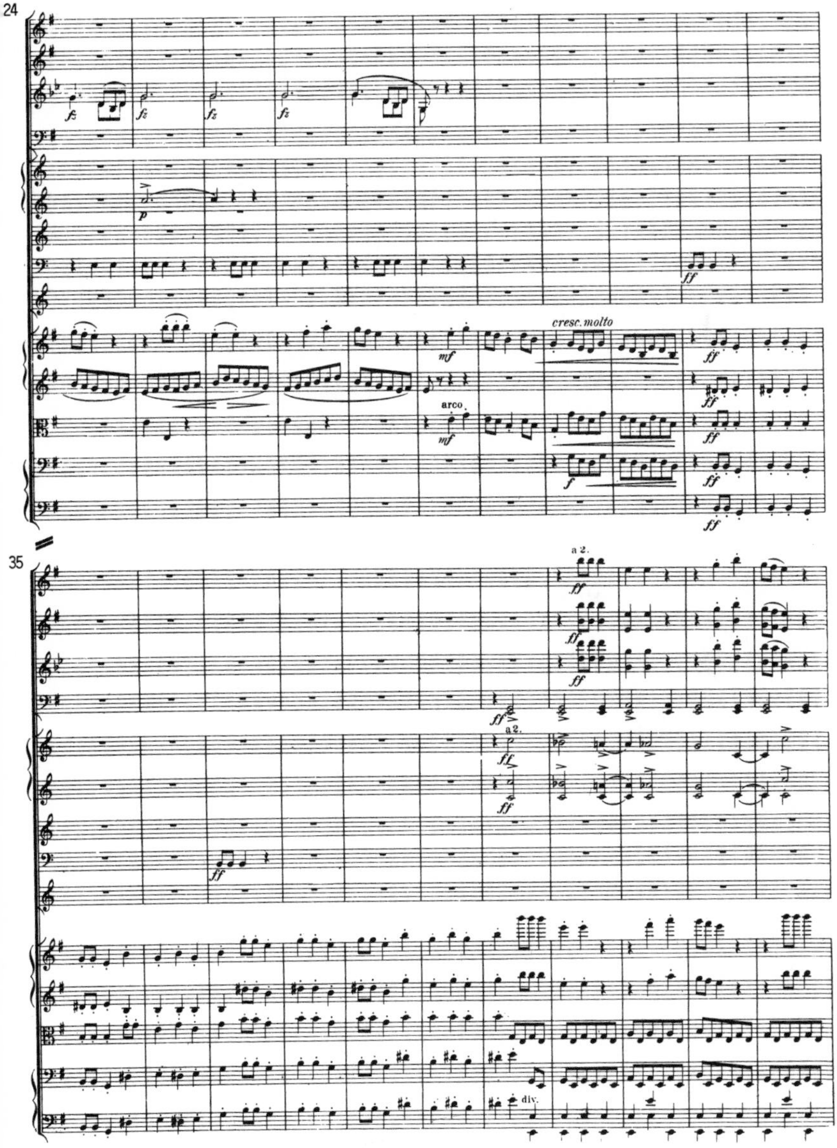
24
fz
p
ff
cresc. molto
mf
arco
f
35
a 2.
ff
div.

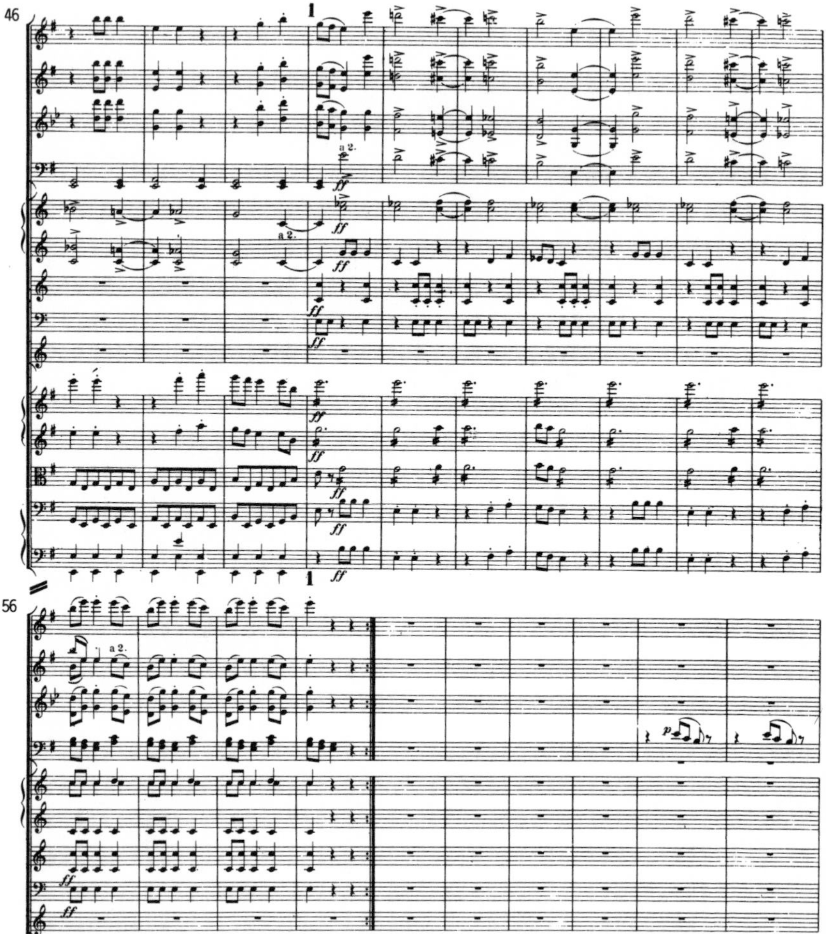
46
1
a 2.
ff
56
fp
p
dim.
pdim.

42

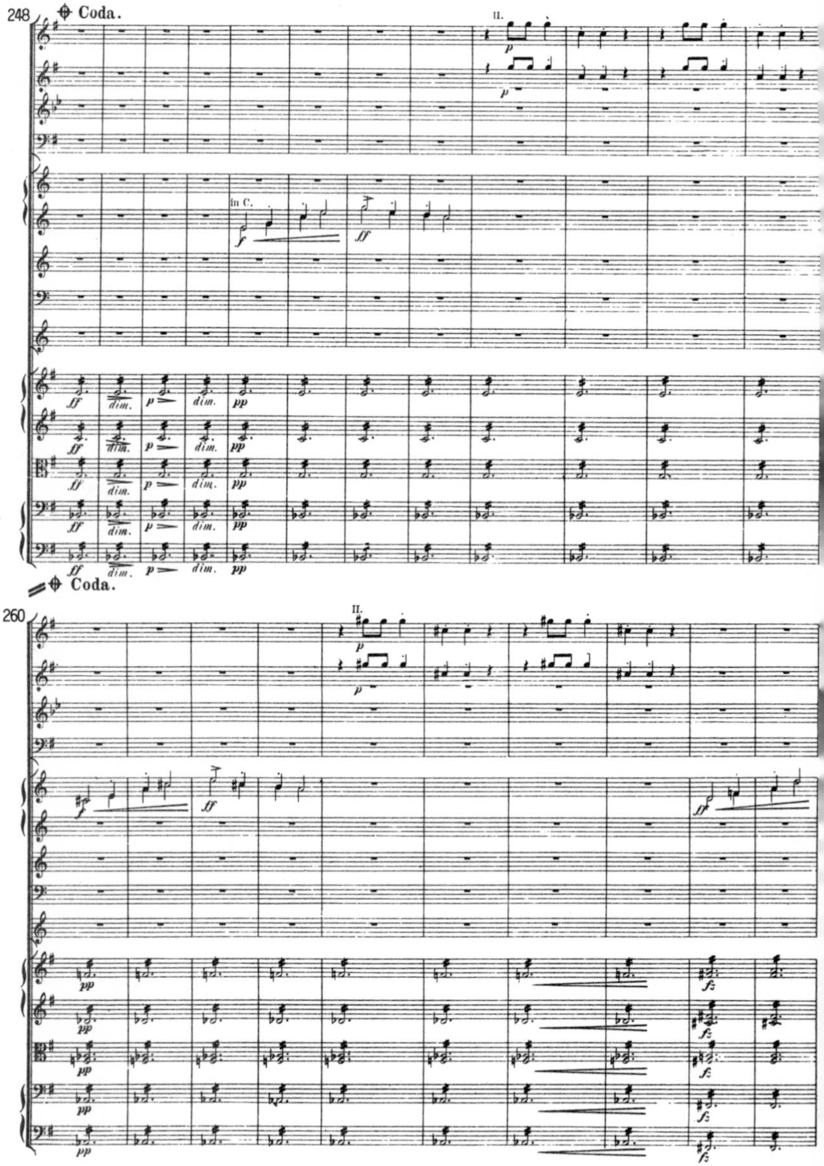
248
Coda.
II.
p
in C.
f
ff
dim.
pp
Coda.
260
II.
p
ff
fz

# IV.

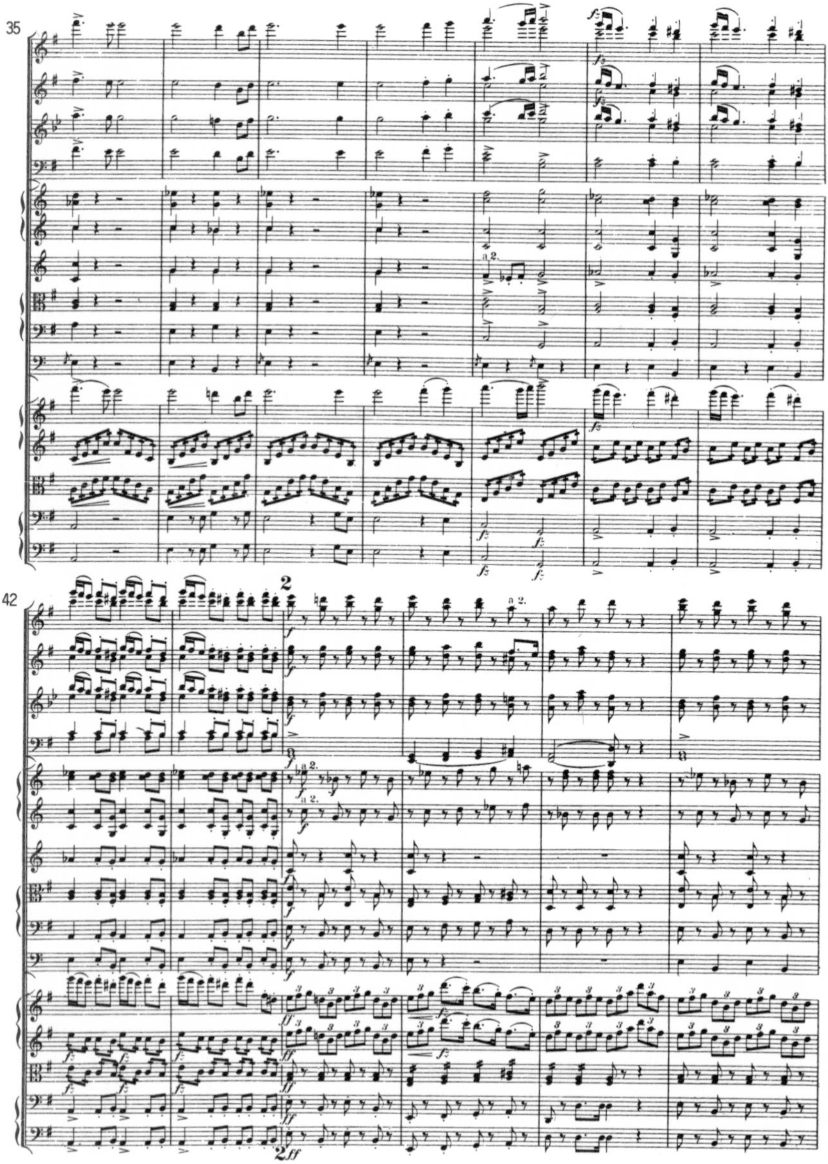
35
42
a 2.
2

55

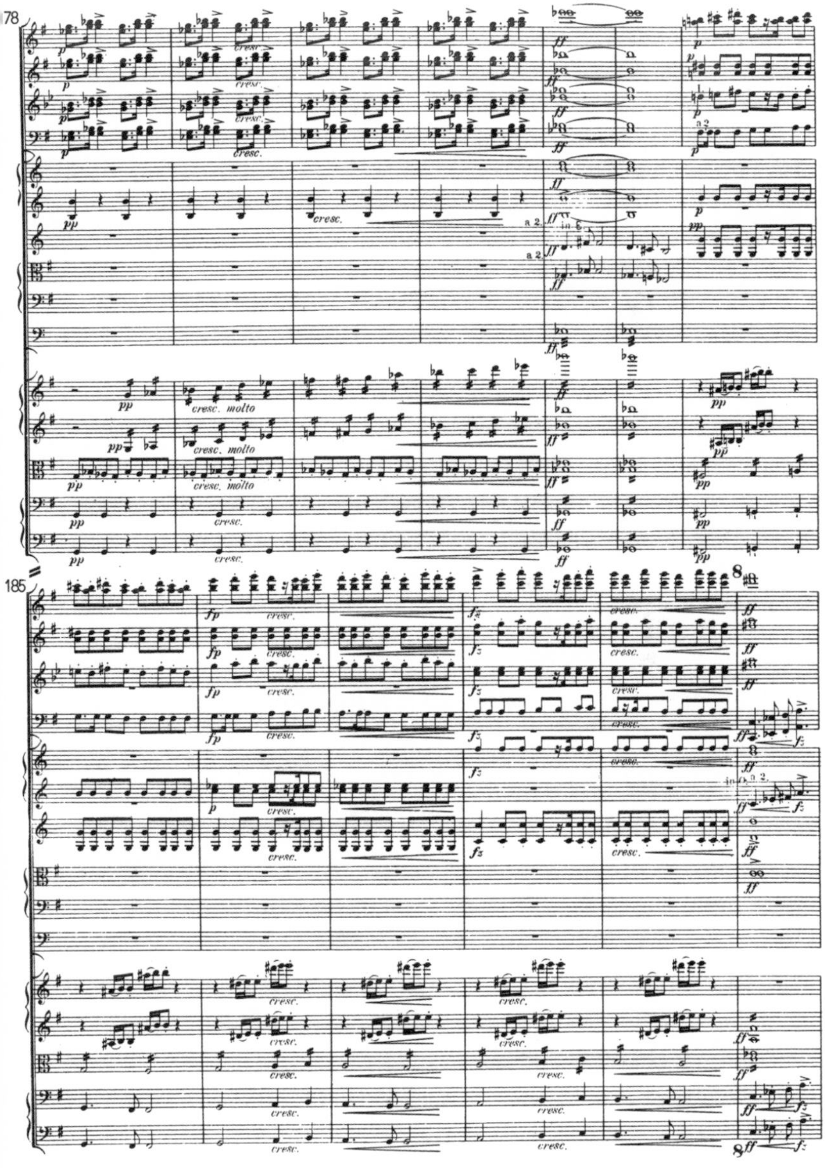
178
cresc.
cresc. molto
a 2
in E
185
8
cresc.

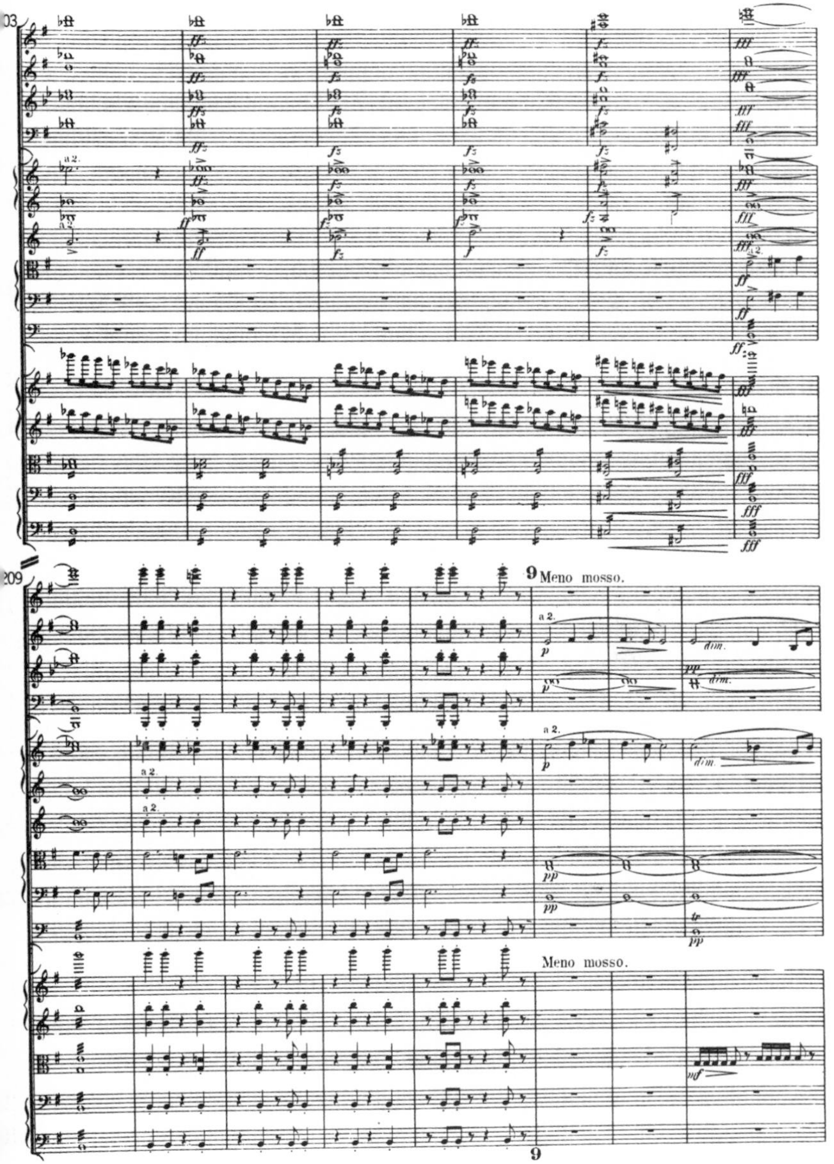
203
a 2.
209
a 2.
9 Meno mosso.
dim.
Meno mosso.
9

68

69

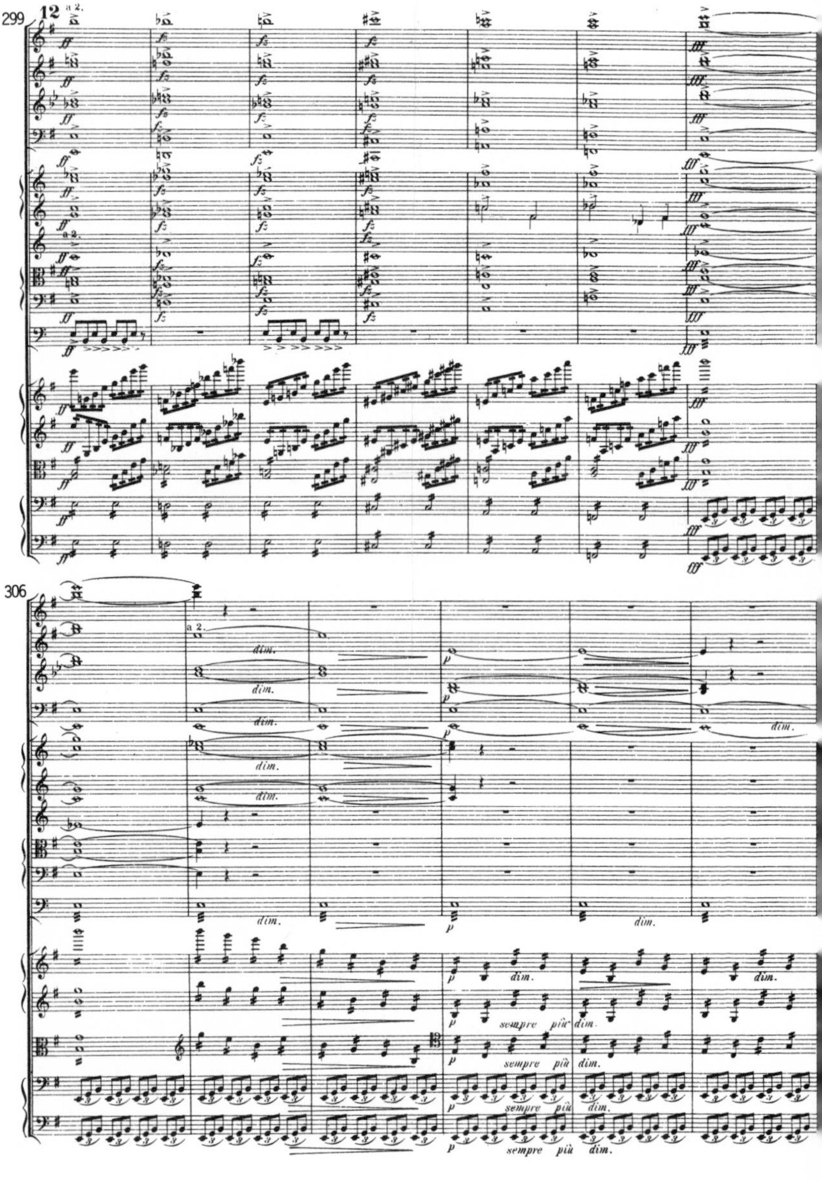

299
12
a 2.
306
a 2.
dim.
sempre più dim.

END OF EDITION